Grandad's password notebook

Keep Track Books

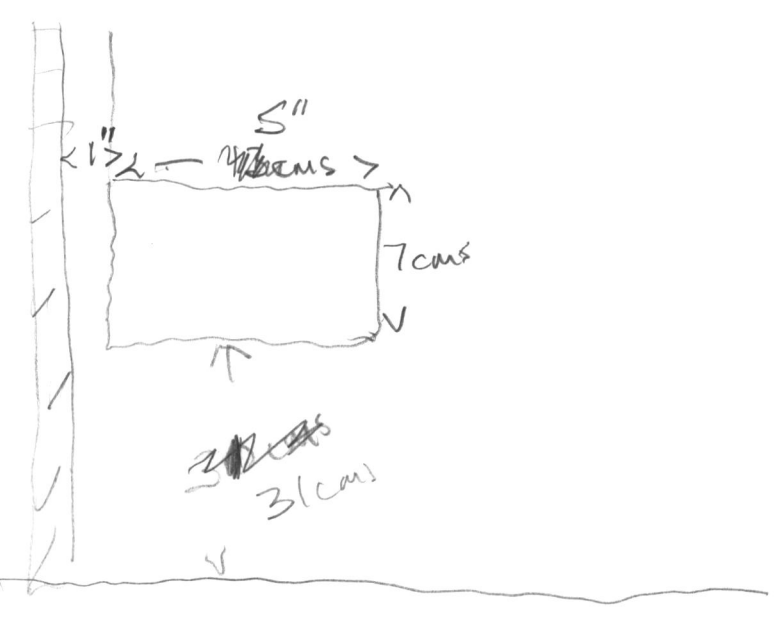

© Keep Track Books

All rights reserved
No part of this publication may be reproduced, stored in a retrieval system, or transmitted in any form or by any means, electronic, mechanical, photocopying, recording or otherwise, without the prior written permission of the copyright owner.

Unauthorised reproduction of any part of this publication by any means including photocopying is an infringement of copyright.

A

Name	Date
Web address	
Username/login	
Password	PIN
Security questions/notes	

Name	Date
Web address	
Username/login	
Password	PIN
Security questions/notes	

Name	Date
Web address	
Username/login	
Password	PIN
Security questions/notes	

Name	Date
Web address	
Username/login	
Password	PIN
Security questions/notes	

Name	Date
Web address	
Username/login	
Password	PIN
Security questions/notes	

Name	Date
Web address	
Username/login	
Password	PIN
Security questions/notes	

A

Name	Date
Web address	
Username/login	
Password	PIN
Security questions/notes	

Name	Date
Web address	
Username/login	
Password	PIN
Security questions/notes	

Name	Date
Web address	
Username/login	
Password	PIN
Security questions/notes	

Name	Date
Web address	
Username/login	
Password	PIN
Security questions/notes	

Name	Date
Web address	
Username/login	
Password	PIN
Security questions/notes	

Name	Date
Web address	
Username/login	
Password	PIN
Security questions/notes	

B

Name	Date
Web address	
Username/login	
Password	PIN
Security questions/notes	

Name	Date
Web address	
Username/login	
Password	PIN
Security questions/notes	

Name	Date
Web address	
Username/login	
Password	PIN
Security questions/notes	

B

Name	Date
Web address	
Username/login	
Password	PIN
Security questions/notes	

Name	Date
Web address	
Username/login	
Password	PIN
Security questions/notes	

Name	Date
Web address	
Username/login	
Password	PIN
Security questions/notes	

B

Name	Date
Web address	
Username/login	
Password	PIN
Security questions/notes	

Name	Date
Web address	
Username/login	
Password	PIN
Security questions/notes	

Name	Date
Web address	
Username/login	
Password	PIN
Security questions/notes	

B

Name	Date
Web address	
Username/login	
Password	PIN
Security questions/notes	

Name	Date
Web address	
Username/login	
Password	PIN
Security questions/notes	

Name	Date
Web address	
Username/login	
Password	PIN
Security questions/notes	

Name	Date
Web address	
Username/login	
Password	PIN
Security questions/notes	

Name	Date
Web address	
Username/login	
Password	PIN
Security questions/notes	

Name	Date
Web address	
Username/login	
Password	PIN
Security questions/notes	

Name	Date
Web address	
Username/login	
Password	PIN
Security questions/notes	

Name	Date
Web address	
Username/login	
Password	PIN
Security questions/notes	

Name	Date
Web address	
Username/login	
Password	PIN
Security questions/notes	

C

Name	Date
Web address	
Username/login	
Password	PIN
Security questions/notes	

Name	Date
Web address	
Username/login	
Password	PIN
Security questions/notes	

Name	Date
Web address	
Username/login	
Password	PIN
Security questions/notes	

C

Name	Date
Web address	
Username/login	
Password	PIN
Security questions/notes	

Name	Date
Web address	
Username/login	
Password	PIN
Security questions/notes	

Name	Date
Web address	
Username/login	
Password	PIN
Security questions/notes	

D

Name	Date
Web address	
Username/login	
Password	PIN
Security questions/notes	

Name	Date
Web address	
Username/login	
Password	PIN
Security questions/notes	

Name	Date
Web address	
Username/login	
Password	PIN
Security questions/notes	

D

Name	Date
Web address	
Username/login	
Password	PIN
Security questions/notes	

Name	Date
Web address	
Username/login	
Password	PIN
Security questions/notes	

Name	Date
Web address	
Username/login	
Password	PIN
Security questions/notes	

D

Name	Date
Web address	
Username/login	
Password	PIN
Security questions/notes	

Name	Date
Web address	
Username/login	
Password	PIN
Security questions/notes	

Name	Date
Web address	
Username/login	
Password	PIN
Security questions/notes	

D

Name	Date
Web address	
Username/login	
Password	PIN
Security questions/notes	

Name	Date
Web address	
Username/login	
Password	PIN
Security questions/notes	

Name	Date
Web address	
Username/login	
Password	PIN
Security questions/notes	

E

Name	Date
Web address	
Username/login	
Password	PIN
Security questions/notes	

Name	Date
Web address	
Username/login	
Password	PIN
Security questions/notes	

Name	Date
Web address	
Username/login	
Password	PIN
Security questions/notes	

Name	Date
Web address	
Username/login	
Password	PIN
Security questions/notes	

Name	Date
Web address	
Username/login	
Password	PIN
Security questions/notes	

Name	Date
Web address	
Username/login	
Password	PIN
Security questions/notes	

E

Name	Date
Web address	
Username/login	
Password	PIN
Security questions/notes	

Name	Date
Web address	
Username/login	
Password	PIN
Security questions/notes	

Name	Date
Web address	
Username/login	
Password	PIN
Security questions/notes	

Name	Date
Web address	
Username/login	
Password	PIN
Security questions/notes	

Name	Date
Web address	
Username/login	
Password	PIN
Security questions/notes	

Name	Date
Web address	
Username/login	
Password	PIN
Security questions/notes	

F

Name	Date
Web address	
Username/login	
Password	PIN
Security questions/notes	

Name	Date
Web address	
Username/login	
Password	PIN
Security questions/notes	

Name	Date
Web address	
Username/login	
Password	PIN
Security questions/notes	

F

Name	Date
Web address	
Username/login	
Password	PIN
Security questions/notes	

Name	Date
Web address	
Username/login	
Password	PIN
Security questions/notes	

Name	Date
Web address	
Username/login	
Password	PIN
Security questions/notes	

F

Name	Date
Web address	
Username/login	
Password	PIN
Security questions/notes	

Name	Date
Web address	
Username/login	
Password	PIN
Security questions/notes	

Name	Date
Web address	
Username/login	
Password	PIN
Security questions/notes	

F

Name	Date
Web address	
Username/login	
Password	PIN
Security questions/notes	

Name	Date
Web address	
Username/login	
Password	PIN
Security questions/notes	

Name	Date
Web address	
Username/login	
Password	PIN
Security questions/notes	

G

Name	Date
Web address	
Username/login	
Password	PIN
Security questions/notes	

Name	Date
Web address	
Username/login	
Password	PIN
Security questions/notes	

Name	Date
Web address	
Username/login	
Password	PIN
Security questions/notes	

Name	Date
Web address	
Username/login	
Password	PIN
Security questions/notes	

Name	Date
Web address	
Username/login	
Password	PIN
Security questions/notes	

Name	Date
Web address	
Username/login	
Password	PIN
Security questions/notes	

G

Name	Date
Web address	
Username/login	
Password	PIN
Security questions/notes	

Name	Date
Web address	
Username/login	
Password	PIN
Security questions/notes	

Name	Date
Web address	
Username/login	
Password	PIN
Security questions/notes	

Name	Date
Web address	
Username/login	
Password	PIN
Security questions/notes	

Name	Date
Web address	
Username/login	
Password	PIN
Security questions/notes	

Name	Date
Web address	
Username/login	
Password	PIN
Security questions/notes	

H

Name	Date
Web address	
Username/login	
Password	PIN
Security questions/notes	

Name	Date
Web address	
Username/login	
Password	PIN
Security questions/notes	

Name	Date
Web address	
Username/login	
Password	PIN
Security questions/notes	

Name	Date
Web address	
Username/login	
Password	PIN
Security questions/notes	

Name	Date
Web address	
Username/login	
Password	PIN
Security questions/notes	

Name	Date
Web address	
Username/login	
Password	PIN
Security questions/notes	

H

Name	Date
Web address	
Username/login	
Password	PIN
Security questions/notes	

Name	Date
Web address	
Username/login	
Password	PIN
Security questions/notes	

Name	Date
Web address	
Username/login	
Password	PIN
Security questions/notes	

Name	Date
Web address	
Username/login	
Password	PIN
Security questions/notes	

Name	Date
Web address	
Username/login	
Password	PIN
Security questions/notes	

Name	Date
Web address	
Username/login	
Password	PIN
Security questions/notes	

1

Name	Date
Web address	
Username/login	
Password	PIN
Security questions/notes	

Name	Date
Web address	
Username/login	
Password	PIN
Security questions/notes	

Name	Date
Web address	
Username/login	
Password	PIN
Security questions/notes	

1	

Name	Date
Web address	
Username/login	
Password	PIN
Security questions/notes	

Name	Date
Web address	
Username/login	
Password	PIN
Security questions/notes	

Name	Date
Web address	
Username/login	
Password	PIN
Security questions/notes	

1

Name	Date
Web address	
Username/login	
Password	PIN
Security questions/notes	

Name	Date
Web address	
Username/login	
Password	PIN
Security questions/notes	

Name	Date
Web address	
Username/login	
Password	PIN
Security questions/notes	

| 1 |

Name	Date
Web address	
Username/login	
Password	PIN
Security questions/notes	

Name	Date
Web address	
Username/login	
Password	PIN
Security questions/notes	

Name	Date
Web address	
Username/login	
Password	PIN
Security questions/notes	

J

Name	Date
Web address	
Username/login	
Password	PIN
Security questions/notes	

Name	Date
Web address	
Username/login	
Password	PIN
Security questions/notes	

Name	Date
Web address	
Username/login	
Password	PIN
Security questions/notes	

J

Name	Date
Web address	
Username/login	
Password	PIN
Security questions/notes	

Name	Date
Web address	
Username/login	
Password	PIN
Security questions/notes	

Name	Date
Web address	
Username/login	
Password	PIN
Security questions/notes	

J

Name	Date
Web address	
Username/login	
Password	PIN
Security questions/notes	

Name	Date
Web address	
Username/login	
Password	PIN
Security questions/notes	

Name	Date
Web address	
Username/login	
Password	PIN
Security questions/notes	

J

Name	Date
Web address	
Username/login	
Password	PIN
Security questions/notes	

Name	Date
Web address	
Username/login	
Password	PIN
Security questions/notes	

Name	Date
Web address	
Username/login	
Password	PIN
Security questions/notes	

K

Name	Date
Web address	
Username/login	
Password	PIN
Security questions/notes	

Name	Date
Web address	
Username/login	
Password	PIN
Security questions/notes	

Name	Date
Web address	
Username/login	
Password	PIN
Security questions/notes	

K

Name	Date
Web address	
Username/login	
Password	PIN
Security questions/notes	

Name	Date
Web address	
Username/login	
Password	PIN
Security questions/notes	

Name	Date
Web address	
Username/login	
Password	PIN
Security questions/notes	

K

Name	Date
Web address	
Username/login	
Password	PIN
Security questions/notes	

Name	Date
Web address	
Username/login	
Password	PIN
Security questions/notes	

Name	Date
Web address	
Username/login	
Password	PIN
Security questions/notes	

Name	Date
Web address	
Username/login	
Password	PIN
Security questions/notes	

Name	Date
Web address	
Username/login	
Password	PIN
Security questions/notes	

Name	Date
Web address	
Username/login	
Password	PIN
Security questions/notes	

L

Name	Date
Web address	
Username/login	
Password	PIN
Security questions/notes	

Name	Date
Web address	
Username/login	
Password	PIN
Security questions/notes	

Name	Date
Web address	
Username/login	
Password	PIN
Security questions/notes	

L

Name	Date
Web address	
Username/login	
Password	PIN
Security questions/notes	

Name	Date
Web address	
Username/login	
Password	PIN
Security questions/notes	

Name	Date
Web address	
Username/login	
Password	PIN
Security questions/notes	

L

Name	Date
Web address	
Username/login	
Password	PIN
Security questions/notes	

Name	Date
Web address	
Username/login	
Password	PIN
Security questions/notes	

Name	Date
Web address	
Username/login	
Password	PIN
Security questions/notes	

L

Name	Date
Web address	
Username/login	
Password	PIN
Security questions/notes	

Name	Date
Web address	
Username/login	
Password	PIN
Security questions/notes	

Name	Date
Web address	
Username/login	
Password	PIN
Security questions/notes	

M

Name	Date
Web address	
Username/login	
Password	PIN
Security questions/notes	

Name	Date
Web address	
Username/login	
Password	PIN
Security questions/notes	

Name	Date
Web address	
Username/login	
Password	PIN
Security questions/notes	

Name	Date
Web address	
Username/login	
Password	PIN
Security questions/notes	

Name	Date
Web address	
Username/login	
Password	PIN
Security questions/notes	

Name	Date
Web address	
Username/login	
Password	PIN
Security questions/notes	

M

Name	Date
Web address	
Username/login	
Password	PIN
Security questions/notes	

Name	Date
Web address	
Username/login	
Password	PIN
Security questions/notes	

Name	Date
Web address	
Username/login	
Password	PIN
Security questions/notes	

Name	Date
Web address	
Username/login	
Password	PIN
Security questions/notes	

Name	Date
Web address	
Username/login	
Password	PIN
Security questions/notes	

Name	Date
Web address	
Username/login	
Password	PIN
Security questions/notes	

N

Name	Date
Web address	
Username/login	
Password	PIN
Security questions/notes	

Name	Date
Web address	
Username/login	
Password	PIN
Security questions/notes	

Name	Date
Web address	
Username/login	
Password	PIN
Security questions/notes	

N

Name	Date
Web address	
Username/login	
Password	PIN
Security questions/notes	

Name	Date
Web address	
Username/login	
Password	PIN
Security questions/notes	

Name	Date
Web address	
Username/login	
Password	PIN
Security questions/notes	

N

Name	Date
Web address	
Username/login	
Password	PIN
Security questions/notes	

Name	Date
Web address	
Username/login	
Password	PIN
Security questions/notes	

Name	Date
Web address	
Username/login	
Password	PIN
Security questions/notes	

N

Name	Date
Web address	
Username/login	
Password	PIN
Security questions/notes	

Name	Date
Web address	
Username/login	
Password	PIN
Security questions/notes	

Name	Date
Web address	
Username/login	
Password	PIN
Security questions/notes	

Name	Date
Web address	
Username/login	
Password	PIN
Security questions/notes	

Name	Date
Web address	
Username/login	
Password	PIN
Security questions/notes	

Name	Date
Web address	
Username/login	
Password	PIN
Security questions/notes	

Name	Date
Web address	
Username/login	
Password	PIN
Security questions/notes	

Name	Date
Web address	
Username/login	
Password	PIN
Security questions/notes	

Name	Date
Web address	
Username/login	
Password	PIN
Security questions/notes	

Name	Date
Web address	
Username/login	
Password	PIN
Security questions/notes	

Name	Date
Web address	
Username/login	
Password	PIN
Security questions/notes	

Name	Date
Web address	
Username/login	
Password	PIN
Security questions/notes	

Name	Date
Web address	
Username/login	
Password	PIN
Security questions/notes	

Name	Date
Web address	
Username/login	
Password	PIN
Security questions/notes	

Name	Date
Web address	
Username/login	
Password	PIN
Security questions/notes	

P

Name	Date
Web address	
Username/login	
Password	PIN
Security questions/notes	

Name	Date
Web address	
Username/login	
Password	PIN
Security questions/notes	

Name	Date
Web address	
Username/login	
Password	PIN
Security questions/notes	

P

Name	Date
Web address	
Username/login	
Password	PIN
Security questions/notes	

Name	Date
Web address	
Username/login	
Password	PIN
Security questions/notes	

Name	Date
Web address	
Username/login	
Password	PIN
Security questions/notes	

P

Name	Date
Web address	
Username/login	
Password	PIN
Security questions/notes	

Name	Date
Web address	
Username/login	
Password	PIN
Security questions/notes	

Name	Date
Web address	
Username/login	
Password	PIN
Security questions/notes	

P

Name	Date
Web address	
Username/login	
Password	PIN
Security questions/notes	

Name	Date
Web address	
Username/login	
Password	PIN
Security questions/notes	

Name	Date
Web address	
Username/login	
Password	PIN
Security questions/notes	

Q

Name	Date
Web address	
Username/login	
Password	PIN
Security questions/notes	

Name	Date
Web address	
Username/login	
Password	PIN
Security questions/notes	

Name	Date
Web address	
Username/login	
Password	PIN
Security questions/notes	

Name	Date
Web address	
Username/login	
Password	PIN
Security questions/notes	

Name	Date
Web address	
Username/login	
Password	PIN
Security questions/notes	

Name	Date
Web address	
Username/login	
Password	PIN
Security questions/notes	

Q

Name	Date
Web address	
Username/login	
Password	PIN
Security questions/notes	

Name	Date
Web address	
Username/login	
Password	PIN
Security questions/notes	

Name	Date
Web address	
Username/login	
Password	PIN
Security questions/notes	

Name	Date
Web address	
Username/login	
Password	PIN
Security questions/notes	

Name	Date
Web address	
Username/login	
Password	PIN
Security questions/notes	

Name	Date
Web address	
Username/login	
Password	PIN
Security questions/notes	

R

Name	Date
Web address	
Username/login	
Password	PIN
Security questions/notes	

Name	Date
Web address	
Username/login	
Password	PIN
Security questions/notes	

Name	Date
Web address	
Username/login	
Password	PIN
Security questions/notes	

R

Name	Date
Web address	
Username/login	
Password	PIN
Security questions/notes	

Name	Date
Web address	
Username/login	
Password	PIN
Security questions/notes	

Name	Date
Web address	
Username/login	
Password	PIN
Security questions/notes	

R

Name	Date
Web address	
Username/login	
Password	PIN
Security questions/notes	

Name	Date
Web address	
Username/login	
Password	PIN
Security questions/notes	

Name	Date
Web address	
Username/login	
Password	PIN
Security questions/notes	

R

Name	Date
Web address	
Username/login	
Password	PIN
Security questions/notes	

Name	Date
Web address	
Username/login	
Password	PIN
Security questions/notes	

Name	Date
Web address	
Username/login	
Password	PIN
Security questions/notes	

S

Name	Date
Web address	
Username/login	
Password	PIN
Security questions/notes	

Name	Date
Web address	
Username/login	
Password	PIN
Security questions/notes	

Name	Date
Web address	
Username/login	
Password	PIN
Security questions/notes	

S

Name	Date
Web address	
Username/login	
Password	PIN
Security questions/notes	

Name	Date
Web address	
Username/login	
Password	PIN
Security questions/notes	

Name	Date
Web address	
Username/login	
Password	PIN
Security questions/notes	

S

Name	Date
Web address	
Username/login	
Password	PIN
Security questions/notes	

Name	Date
Web address	
Username/login	
Password	PIN
Security questions/notes	

Name	Date
Web address	
Username/login	
Password	PIN
Security questions/notes	

S

Name	Date
Web address	
Username/login	
Password	PIN
Security questions/notes	

Name	Date
Web address	
Username/login	
Password	PIN
Security questions/notes	

Name	Date
Web address	
Username/login	
Password	PIN
Security questions/notes	

T

Name	Date
Web address	
Username/login	
Password	PIN
Security questions/notes	

Name	Date
Web address	
Username/login	
Password	PIN
Security questions/notes	

Name	Date
Web address	
Username/login	
Password	PIN
Security questions/notes	

| T |

Name	Date
Web address	
Username/login	
Password	PIN
Security questions/notes	

Name	Date
Web address	
Username/login	
Password	PIN
Security questions/notes	

Name	Date
Web address	
Username/login	
Password	PIN
Security questions/notes	

T

Name	Date
Web address	
Username/login	
Password	PIN
Security questions/notes	

Name	Date
Web address	
Username/login	
Password	PIN
Security questions/notes	

Name	Date
Web address	
Username/login	
Password	PIN
Security questions/notes	

T

Name	Date
Web address	
Username/login	
Password	PIN
Security questions/notes	

Name	Date
Web address	
Username/login	
Password	PIN
Security questions/notes	

Name	Date
Web address	
Username/login	
Password	PIN
Security questions/notes	

| U |

Name	Date
Web address	
Username/login	
Password	PIN
Security questions/notes	

Name	Date
Web address	
Username/login	
Password	PIN
Security questions/notes	

Name	Date
Web address	
Username/login	
Password	PIN
Security questions/notes	

Name	Date
Web address	
Username/login	
Password	PIN
Security questions/notes	

Name	Date
Web address	
Username/login	
Password	PIN
Security questions/notes	

Name	Date
Web address	
Username/login	
Password	PIN
Security questions/notes	

U

Name	Date
Web address	
Username/login	
Password	PIN
Security questions/notes	

Name	Date
Web address	
Username/login	
Password	PIN
Security questions/notes	

Name	Date
Web address	
Username/login	
Password	PIN
Security questions/notes	

Name	Date
Web address	
Username/login	
Password	PIN
Security questions/notes	

Name	Date
Web address	
Username/login	
Password	PIN
Security questions/notes	

Name	Date
Web address	
Username/login	
Password	PIN
Security questions/notes	

V

Name	Date
Web address	
Username/login	
Password	PIN
Security questions/notes	

Name	Date
Web address	
Username/login	
Password	PIN
Security questions/notes	

Name	Date
Web address	
Username/login	
Password	PIN
Security questions/notes	

Name	Date
Web address	
Username/login	
Password	PIN
Security questions/notes	

Name	Date
Web address	
Username/login	
Password	PIN
Security questions/notes	

Name	Date
Web address	
Username/login	
Password	PIN
Security questions/notes	

V

Name	Date
Web address	
Username/login	
Password	PIN
Security questions/notes	

Name	Date
Web address	
Username/login	
Password	PIN
Security questions/notes	

Name	Date
Web address	
Username/login	
Password	PIN
Security questions/notes	

Name	Date
Web address	
Username/login	
Password	PIN
Security questions/notes	

Name	Date
Web address	
Username/login	
Password	PIN
Security questions/notes	

Name	Date
Web address	
Username/login	
Password	PIN
Security questions/notes	

W

Name	Date
Web address	
Username/login	
Password	PIN
Security questions/notes	

Name	Date
Web address	
Username/login	
Password	PIN
Security questions/notes	

Name	Date
Web address	
Username/login	
Password	PIN
Security questions/notes	

Name	Date
Web address	
Username/login	
Password	PIN
Security questions/notes	

Name	Date
Web address	
Username/login	
Password	PIN
Security questions/notes	

Name	Date
Web address	
Username/login	
Password	PIN
Security questions/notes	

W

Name	Date
Web address	
Username/login	
Password	PIN
Security questions/notes	

Name	Date
Web address	
Username/login	
Password	PIN
Security questions/notes	

Name	Date
Web address	
Username/login	
Password	PIN
Security questions/notes	

Name	Date
Web address	
Username/login	
Password	PIN
Security questions/notes	

Name	Date
Web address	
Username/login	
Password	PIN
Security questions/notes	

Name	Date
Web address	
Username/login	
Password	PIN
Security questions/notes	

		X

Name	Date
Web address	
Username/login	
Password	PIN
Security questions/notes	

Name	Date
Web address	
Username/login	
Password	PIN
Security questions/notes	

Name	Date
Web address	
Username/login	
Password	PIN
Security questions/notes	

Name	Date
Web address	
Username/login	
Password	PIN
Security questions/notes	

Name	Date
Web address	
Username/login	
Password	PIN
Security questions/notes	

Name	Date
Web address	
Username/login	
Password	PIN
Security questions/notes	

Y

Name	Date
Web address	
Username/login	
Password	PIN
Security questions/notes	

Name	Date
Web address	
Username/login	
Password	PIN
Security questions/notes	

Name	Date
Web address	
Username/login	
Password	PIN
Security questions/notes	

Y

Name	Date
Web address	
Username/login	
Password	PIN
Security questions/notes	

Name	Date
Web address	
Username/login	
Password	PIN
Security questions/notes	

Name	Date
Web address	
Username/login	
Password	PIN
Security questions/notes	

Y

Name	Date
Web address	
Username/login	
Password	PIN
Security questions/notes	

Name	Date
Web address	
Username/login	
Password	PIN
Security questions/notes	

Name	Date
Web address	
Username/login	
Password	PIN
Security questions/notes	

Y

Name	Date
Web address	
Username/login	
Password	PIN
Security questions/notes	

Name	Date
Web address	
Username/login	
Password	PIN
Security questions/notes	

Name	Date
Web address	
Username/login	
Password	PIN
Security questions/notes	

Z

Name	Date
Web address	
Username/login	
Password	PIN
Security questions/notes	

Name	Date
Web address	
Username/login	
Password	PIN
Security questions/notes	

Name	Date
Web address	
Username/login	
Password	PIN
Security questions/notes	

Z

Name	Date
Web address	
Username/login	
Password	PIN
Security questions/notes	

Name	Date
Web address	
Username/login	
Password	PIN
Security questions/notes	

Name	Date
Web address	
Username/login	
Password	PIN
Security questions/notes	

Keep Track Books brings you
a variety of essential notebooks —
including password notebooks
with the same interior as this one,
but with different cover designs.

Visit
www.lusciousbooks.co.uk
to discover more notebooks.

Printed in Great Britain
by Amazon